Portland Community
W9-CUA-669

CUTTING-EDGE STEM CAREERS™

TOP STEM CAREERS IN ENGINEERING

GINA HAGLER

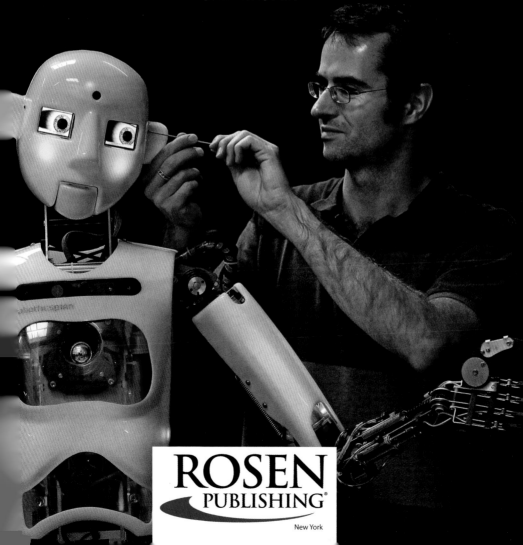

ROSEN
PUBLISHING®
New York

Published in 2015 by The Rosen Publishing Group, Inc.
29 East 21st Street, New York, NY 10010

Copyright © 2015 by The Rosen Publishing Group, Inc.

First Edition

All rights reserved. No part of this book may be reproduced in any form without permission in writing from the publisher, except by a reviewer.

Library of Congress Cataloging-in-Publication Data

Hagler, Gina.
Top STEM careers in engineering/Gina Hagler.—
First edition.
    pages cm—(Cutting-edge STEM careers)
Audience: Grades 9-12.
Includes bibliographical references and index.
ISBN 978-1-4777-7672-8 (library bound)—
ISBN 978-1-4777-7674-2 (pbk.)—
ISBN 978-1-4777-7675-9 (6-pack)
1. Engineering—Vocational guidance—Juvenile literature. 2. Technology—Vocational guidance—Juvenile literature. I. Title.
TA157.H245 2015
620.0023—dc23

                                        2013039267

Manufactured in Malaysia

CONTENTS

China's Three Gorges Dam is the world's largest hydroelectric facility. Engineers from many disciplines consulted on this project.

There are so many interesting careers to choose from. It can be difficult to narrow in on the one that's just right for you. Each possible career involves a slightly different skill set applied in a different set of circumstances. Some careers weigh heavily on writing ability. Some require a stringent education in the sciences. Others call for comforting people during difficult times.

Engineering careers require a thorough education and success in the STEM fields: science, technology, engineering, and mathematics. Because STEM professionals work in fields that require a rigorous course of study, they are well compensated and in great demand. But engineering is not just about manipulating numbers and applying scientific principles. Engineering professionals blend precision with imagination, and numbers and figures with vision and foresight, to create solutions for some of the most pressing problems facing humankind today.

Some of the problems engineers are called upon to solve impact millions of people. This was the case when the Chinese government faced the problem of recurring flooding of the Yangtze River in eastern China. To solve this problem, it turned to engineers from around the world for a solution. The engineers were tasked with solving the problem of flooding. Each year when the Yangtze River overflowed its banks, the result was widespread devastation and death throughout the region. The flooding disrupted trade, interfered with farming activities, and caused a significant loss of life. Clearly something needed to be done. Many options were considered, but in the end it was decided that a mammoth dam—the Three Gorges Dam—would be built near the town of Sandouping in mainland China's Hubei Province.

To undertake a project of this size was no small matter. According to *China Daily*, the monetary estimate for the project was 180 billion yuan, or more than $20 billion. Entire towns had to be relocated because of permanent flooding that would result when the reservoir behind the dam filled, causing those historical sites to be lost forever. On the positive side, there would be a renewable source of power for millions of people. There would also be a way for large ships to regularly reach inland portions of China for the first time in history.

Engineers were essential to this project. These professionals determined the environmental impact of the dam—including loss of habitat, loss of species, potential for earthquake activity, and creation of silt—and set about finding ways to minimize these effects. They had to ensure that the design was good (i.e., it wouldn't fail and cause catastrophic flooding throughout the region) and that it was capable of being implemented successfully. They also had to be certain that it would solve the flooding problem while generating sufficient energy for the growing population in need of power. Finally, they had to ensure that the dam would create the conditions necessary for cargo vessels to reach farther inland than ever before.

Engineers were essential to the Three Gorges Dam project because they had the technical knowledge to back up their findings and recommendations with hard science. They weren't guessing when they provided the specifications for the dam and its components. They could use their knowledge as the foundation for their suggestions and plans. Their specifications were based on thorough model testing. Their knowledge also helped them predict the behavior of the land around the dam, both during construction and after the dam's completion. It was this combination of theoretical and practical knowledge, along with experience, that made engineers the right professionals for the project.

Many different kinds of engineers played vital roles in the project. Civil and environmental engineers assessed the potential for damage to the environment and figured out how the dam should be situated for maximum performance. Chemical engineers assessed the materials to be used, and mechanical engineers worked on the moving parts of the project. Electrical and computer engineers designed systems to power and control the workings of the dam.

Working as a team, engineers met the stated need to prevent flooding. They incorporated a clean source of energy—hydroelectric power—for a growing economy, while improving shipping options on the Yangtze River. Ultimately, the Three Gorges Dam was a monumental engineering success.

Not all engineering projects are as large as the Three Gorges Dam, but even the smallest projects have an impact on the people and places involved. Whether you choose to be a biomedical engineer creating a prosthetic leg for someone who has lost a limb, a chemical engineer identifying new sources of fuel, or a mechanical engineer designing a robotic arm for a new space probe, a rewarding career in engineering is your ultimate goal.

In the pages that follow, we will explore each of these branches of engineering. We will discuss the educational requirements, types of work available, and typical workplaces for these professionals. We will also take a look at some real-life examples of engineering at work. Lastly, we will discuss what it takes to get started and stay current in these rapidly changing disciplines.

CHAPTER ONE

Engineering as a Career

A career in engineering combines strong math and science skills with creativity and problem-solving skills. "Engineering is a profession centered on creative problem-solving and making things work," said Stuart S. Nielsen, PE, in an interview with the author. A methods engineer for the Office of Bridges and Structures at the Iowa Department of Transportation, Nielsen has spent his career in bridge design and the creation of statewide standards for bridges.

Not all engineers are civil engineers who work on civic projects like bridges. Some engineers work with people in medical fields to create bionics and prosthetics. Other engineers work to convert chemicals into useful materials by pioneering new processing techniques. Electrical and computer engineers focus on energy needs and circuitry for the wide

Sometimes an engineer is called upon to inspect structures far above or below the ground. Here, an engineer inspects the exterior of the Washington Monument in Washington, D.C.

range of electronic equipment that we use each day. Mechanical engineers focus on the design and manufacture of motorized systems that have revolutionized entire factories.

All of these types of engineers must have a thorough understanding of scientific, technological, and mathematical principles and how to apply them to the problems being solved. Much engineering work involves the formulation of new approaches. Work related to existing structures and technologies often calls for innovative approaches that take advantage of technological advances.

Engineers are in high demand. They are well compensated and do interesting and meaningful work. To qualify for this work, they must first complete a stringent course of study.

Educational Requirements

Preparation for a career in engineering begins in high school. Students interested in pursuing a college degree in engineering complete a number of upper-level math and science courses. These courses include calculus and trigonometry. They also include physics, often at the Advanced Placement (AP) level. Some high schools have programs specifically designed for students who want to pursue careers in STEM fields. Even if your high school doesn't, you can still take any advanced coursework offered at your school. In addition, you can explore the possibilities for advanced study offered by your local community college.

A student makes adjustments to his hybrid car during the Intel International Science and Engineering Fair.

High school students can show their interest in, and prepare for a degree in, engineering by participating in extracurricular activities that focus on STEM subjects. This might mean taking part in a NASA competition to design a space city, joining the future aviators club to learn more about flight, or participating in a robotics club and challenge.

Participating in science fairs and contests is an excellent way to prepare for an engineering career and make yourself a more attractive candidate for college-level engineering programs. The Intel International Science and Engineering Fair (Intel ISEF) is the largest scientific research event in the world for those in grades 9 through 12. The awards include scholarships, tuition grants, internships, and scientific field trips. Your guidance counselor can help you learn more about the series of science fairs that lead to participation in this highly regarded competition.

Local engineering firms and national engineering organizations may have opportunities for you to learn more about engineering careers. You can contact these firms and organizations for information about internships or volunteer opportunities. Your guidance counselor, career counselor, librarian, or other adult can also help you identify the resources you need.

College

You may be surprised at the number of specific engineering majors available to you when you enter college. You'll find majors in biomedical engineering, chemical engineering, civil engineering, environmental

THE FE, THE PE, AND THE LICENSING PROCESS

For many professionals, there are licensing or other certification exams that bring advantages to those who pass them. For accounting professionals, the Certified Public Accountant (CPA) exam is critical. For psychotherapists, the designation of Licensed Clinical Social Worker (LCSW) is important. For those pursuing careers in engineering, the Professional Engineer (PE) license brings key professional benefits.

Professional exams for engineers and surveyors are developed, administered, and scored by the National Council of Examiners for Engineering and Surveying (NCEES). An engineer who has earned the designation of PE can stamp and seal designs, bid for government contracts, be principal of a firm, perform consulting services, and offer services to the public. Each of these activities is an important part of a thriving and satisfying career as an engineer.

There are four steps necessary to earn a PE license and the recognition of professional achievement that it brings:

1. Earn an engineering degree from an accredited engineering program.
2. Pass the Fundamentals of Engineering (FE) exam, also known as the Engineer in Training (EIT) exam, while completing the requirements for a bachelor's degree. This exam is made up of two parts: The first, given in the morning, consists of 120 questions that all candidates must answer; the second, given in the afternoon, is made up of 60

questions that relate to areas of specialization, such as civil, chemical, electrical, or mechanical engineering.

3. Attain a minimum of four years of work experience under the supervision of a licensed PE.

4. Pass the PE exam for a specialty area. This eight-hour exam is split between morning and afternoon sessions. Test-takers are provided with surveying reference materials on exam day. Specifics for each specialty area can be found on the NCEES Web site, at http://ncees.org. This information is very useful when preparing for the exam.

The NCEES maintains complete information on the licensing process. It also publishes study materials and offers information related to all aspects of the examination process. Remember to also check with state authorities to see if there are any requirements specific to your state.

engineering, electrical engineering, computer engineering, and mechanical engineering—just to name a few. Some requirements are the same for all engineering majors, while others vary by field. Your first year of engineering coursework is likely to be general in nature and fulfill the requirements for several majors. This gives you the opportunity to explore the different disciplines and participate in some of the clubs and activities related to them.

By the time you are in your junior year, you will probably find that research opportunities are open to you. Even if you're not planning to become a researcher,

These ninth-grade girls learned engineering concepts at a program sponsored by their local university. They subjected their handmade structures to simulated earthquakes.

these can give you a taste of the type of work you will be doing in engineering. The research often centers on innovative approaches to a problem, the use of new materials, or the use of existing materials in new ways.

Take advantage of all the engineering-related opportunities at the college level. Compete in science competitions. Become a student member of an engineering society or Engineers Without Borders. Take the time to read engineering quarterlies in your area of interest. The more you discover, the more comfortable you will be when it comes time to focus on one area of engineering.

Tuition

An engineering degree is not inexpensive. You will need to attend a college or university with a respected program if you expect to move on to a graduate program. That doesn't mean you need to go to the most expensive school in the country. It does mean you will want to pursue a degree at a school with a good reputation and track record for placing its students in graduate programs.

What do you do if this is not financially within your reach? Attend an affordable university and pursue the engineering degree available. Make sure that you are part of a national organization from the start. Make it your business to find a student chapter of the Institute of Electrical and Electronics Engineers (IEEE) or other engineering associations. Find a way to work on research projects in engineering fields. Search out an internship for the summer. Not everything comes to you. Sometimes you have to go out and find what you need.

It's also possible that you will qualify for a grant or scholarship. Be sure to check out what Intel has to offer: one of the most recent winners grew the samples for her experiments in containers under her bed! See if there are regional or national engineering societies that are conducting contests or fairs with tuition or scholarships as prizes.

In addition, many schools offer work-study programs. Some offer paid research opportunities. If you have the grades and test scores required to make you an attractive candidate for a program, a school that wants you may create a way to make it possible for you to attend.

Graduate Study and Licensing

It is becoming increasingly common for engineering professionals to pursue a graduate degree. These degrees are in specialty areas and often include a research component. Graduate work gives you the experience you need for the job you want once you earn your master of science (MS) degree.

Choosing a graduate program is a bit different from choosing an undergraduate program. Very often, you will need to identify the type of work that is being conducted at different institutions and by specific faculty members. The goal is to find an individual with whom you would like to work in a particular specialty. Because of this, your search for the best graduate school depends on the work you plan to do in the future.

By preparing yourself with rigorous mathematics and science coursework, you will be ready to apply to college engineering programs. Once accepted, you'll have a chance to get your feet wet and start working on the general requirements of an engineering degree while learning more about the specific majors. By the time you're ready to head off to graduate school, you'll likely have a clear idea of the work you want to do in the future.

Licensing is another important part of a career as an engineer. The Professional Engineer designation is awarded after completion of the PE exam. There are several other requirements that make up this designation. It is important for you to be aware of these requirements and work to attain this designation if it is called for in the career you envision.

CHAPTER TWO

Biomedical Engineers

Biomedical engineering blends engineering principles and technology with the medical field. Biomedical engineers use their knowledge and expertise to find solutions to problems in biology and medicine. When they succeed, they improve patients' health care and quality of life by extending their capabilities and adding years to their lives.

Biomedical engineers research and develop replacements for body parts, including artificial organs and artificial limbs. They also design the machines used for diagnosing medical problems. They develop the software needed to run the sophisticated equipment used in medical testing and put their knowledge to use in the development of new drug therapies. Some biomedical engineers use their background in mathematics and statistics to build models of systems such as the brain and heart.

A bionic hand allows this man to play an electronic keyboard. A biomedical engineer developed the bionic limb.

Educational Requirements and Licenses

A career in biomedical engineering requires a thorough knowledge of both engineering and biology. In addition, strong communication and mathematics skills are essential.

High School

To be successful in this challenging field requires an understanding of biology, engineering principles, and mathematics, and the ability to produce drawings of new designs and equipment. To achieve this, students in high school are advised to pursue a rigorous course of study that includes upper-level biology, chemistry, life sciences, and  mathematics classes. Specific classes include calculus and physics.

Good communication skills are also important. Students can demonstrate their ability in this area by participating in extracurricular activities and taking honors or advanced English courses.

Students learn to use biotechnology equipment in a lab program designed for interested students at the high school and college levels.

College

In addition to the general requirements for the bachelor of science (BS) in engineering, candidates for a biomedical engineering degree must complete coursework in biology and chemistry. Requirements include courses on molecules and cells, cells and the cardiovascular system, and neural systems. These classes are vital to biomedical engineers because they must understand the way that body systems work—together and alone—at the most basic levels. Without this understanding, it is not possible to design artificial devices and systems to meet the needs of patients.

Biomedical engineering candidates also complete coursework in statistical mechanics and thermodynamics. The devices that biomedical engineers design often have moving parts and are subject to stress and changes in temperature while in use. To design bionics and prosthetics that will perform well, the engineer must be able to evaluate their performance in models and tests, as well as in actual use.

Depending on the kind of work they plan to do, candidates for the BS in biomedical engineering may take additional courses in the design of machinery or computer programming. This knowledge will help them complete their work tasks and communicate effectively with the other engineers at work on a project.

Students with an interest in this field may pursue a BS in biomedical engineering or a BS in engineering with a specialty in biomedical engineering. The difference is in the required courses and the focus of the undergraduate degree.

Graduate Study

As is the case with most engineering degrees, it is often necessary to attain a graduate degree in biomedical engineering. This is especially true if a career in research, medicine, or academics is the goal. For some biomedical engineers, the graduate degree may be where most of the specialization occurs, especially if one elects to earn a bachelor's degree in engineering rather than biomedical engineering. For others, the graduate degree offers a chance to work with a particular individual or on a specific application that is of interest to the candidate.

Graduate students may assist in research on topics such as drug delivery; the use of nanomaterials; molecular, cellular, and tissue engineering; and biomechanics. Other areas of study may include systems physiology, biosensors, and the use of biomaterials.

A graduate degree in biomedical engineering provides future engineers with an understanding of the interplay between different biological and physical systems. While pursuing a master's degree in biomedical engineering, candidates also become familiar with the methods and protocols used to test new designs in this field.

Licensing and Professional Associations

It is not enough to graduate with a degree in biomedical engineering. Candidates must also pass licensing exams to be certified as a professional engineer.

The Fundamentals of Engineering (FE) exam is the first exam you must take. After passing the FE, you must work for four years in the field before you are eligible to sit for the Principles and Practice of Engineering exam. Once you have passed this, you will have proven your qualifications as an engineer and will become a licensed Professional Engineer (PE).

The Biomedical Engineering Society (BMES) has student chapters at many universities. Participating in the organization's activities and taking advantage of the information it provides will make you aware of licensing requirements that apply to you, as well as internships and other opportunities.

Biomedical Engineers at Work

Biomedical engineers are in high demand. Their unique skill set enables them to choose a career in a workplace that suits them best.

Job Opportunities

Job opportunities for biomedical engineers are most often found in the medical field. Their work results in advances in systems and treatments available to patients with a variety of medical needs.

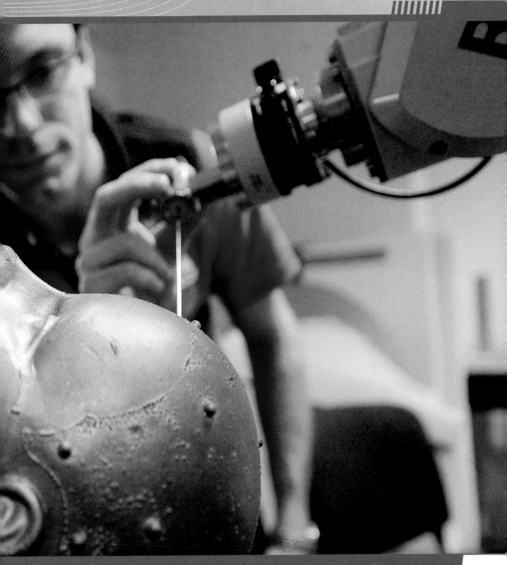

An engineer checks a robotic arm that will someday help surgeons perform brain operations.

Job opportunities include positions in cellular, tissue, genetic, clinical, and rehabilitation engineering. Within these areas, engineers work with

BIONICS: WEARABLE ROBOTS

The Merriam-Webster dictionary defines bionics as "a science concerned with the application of data about the functioning of biological systems to the solution of engineering problems." Biomedical engineers working in the field of bionics create products ranging from wearable robotics to surgical robotics.

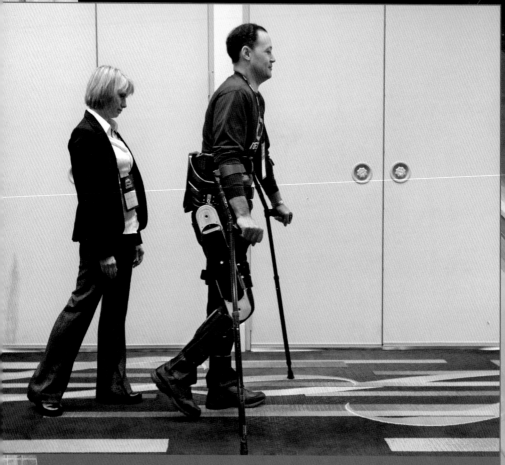

Michael Gore, who is paralyzed from the waist down, walks with the assistance of the Indego Exoskeleton wearable robot.

Just what is a wearable robot? It depends. One type is a complex yet lightweight wearable device that assists someone who is paralyzed to walk on his or her own. The Indego Exoskeleton from Parker Hannifin Corporation is one such wearable robot. It is currently under testing at U.S. rehabilitation hospitals for potential use with disabled veterans.

When wearing the Indego Exoskeleton, slight movement from an individual with a spinal injury is all that is needed to put the robotic device into action. Leaning forward initiates a first step. Tilting from side to side causes the walking motion. Leaning backward brings the device to a stop. With crutches to maintain balance, the person wearing the robotic device is able to get around without a wheelchair.

Wearable robots such as the Indego Exoskeleton are not speedy, so they can't completely take the place of wheelchairs. They do not prevent accidental falls. They are mainly intended for short-term use, to aid in rehabilitation and personal mobility. However, Michael Gore, a person with spinal cord damage who demonstrated the Indego at a 2013 meeting of the American Spinal Injury Association, told the Associated Press, "Being able to speak with you eye-to-eye is just a big emotional boost. Being able to walk up to you and say hello is not a big thing until you cannot do it."

As companies around the world work to perfect competing designs, these and other wearable robotic products are becoming less bulky. They are also likely to come down in price and show improvements in function. The people behind these innovations are people who have chosen careers in biomedical engineering.

bioinstrumentation, biomaterials, and biomechanics. They investigate drug design and delivery and medical imaging. Opportunities in orthopedic surgery, pharmaceuticals, and systems physiology are also available to those with a degree in biomedical engineering.

Workplaces

Biomedical engineers are typically people who enjoy inventing and working with their hands. These engineers also work closely with the people who are the recipients of their work. Because of this, many biomedical engineers are employed in a health care setting such as a hospital, health clinic, or community health organization. During the course of the day, they often research design strategies, create samples of their designs, and speak with the health professionals who use their designs to better understand any improvements that are needed. Biomedical engineers also investigate manufacturing processes to see what is necessary to bring a design to mass production.

Some biomedical engineers work for private companies. In their roles as researchers and designers, they meet with medical professionals to determine any unmet needs (such as a better design in a surgical laser) and then set out to meet that need. Work on such a project may involve people from other disciplines. It may mean working as part of a team, meeting with others in and out of the office, and visiting health care providers to get a better understanding of the current equipment.

Other biomedical engineers are involved in research at universities and research centers, such as the National Institutes of Health (NIH). Their experiments may lead to the development of artificial organs or other products that meet the needs of patients.

Whatever the specific work environment and tasks, biomedical engineers apply technology to the medical field, producing equipment and devices that improve and prolong human life.

Chemical Engineers

Chemical engineering puts an understanding of chemical processes to use in the creation of engineering solutions to a variety of problems. Chemical engineers work on issues ranging from the mitigation of air pollution to the search for new materials for the construction of semiconductors. They work on the design and development of chemical manufacturing equipment, processes, and products, as well as in the development of new drugs and medications and the processes for the production of these substances.

Chemical engineers have an important role to play in the production of biofuels. The process of turning biomass in the form of a crop such as corn into a fuel such as ethanol is all about chemistry. But chemical engineers are not only involved in the search for new, renewable sources of fuel. They are also involved in the search for more efficient methods of clearing oil spills in sensitive areas, the mitigation of a variety of sources of pollution, and the development of products in the pharmaceutical industry.

Educational Requirements and Licenses

Chemical engineers must master coursework in all branches of science. They must also be proficient in engineering concepts that relate to phase changes and chemical processes.

High School

As is the case with other engineering specialties, the preparation for an engineering career begins in earnest during the high school years. Those seeking a place in an undergraduate engineering program must show that they have the required background in mathematics and science, particularly in chemistry. They must also demonstrate that they have the ability to successfully pursue a rigorous course of study.

The best way to demonstrate this is to take upper-level mathematics and science classes. This means taking courses such as AP chemistry, AP calculus, and honors or AP English classes. It also means participating in extracurricular activities related to chemistry and engineering. Participation in science clubs, volunteering at local labs, and doing science fair projects that explore hypotheses based on chemical principles are all viable options for building a portfolio for college.

Goggles on, high school students perform chromatography experiments with grape Kool-Aid during a chemistry summer program.

Investigate the resources that are available to you. If your high school does not have the necessary resources, ask your guidance counselor which national organizations for engineering or chemical engineering you should

contact. Even if none are geared toward students at your level, don't hesitate to contact the associations for advice on how you might find an apprenticeship or mentor to help you in your quest for a career in chemical engineering.

College

Students interested in a career in chemical engineering can pursue a degree in chemical engineering or an engineering degree with a specialization in chemistry. Whichever path is chosen, a strong foundation in mathematics, chemistry, biology, physics, and engineering principles is required.

Coursework typically includes classes in thermodynamics, heat transfer, mass and energy balances, kinetics, fluids, and mass transfer, including phase equilibria and continuous vapor-liquid contractors. Many of the upper-level classes involve lab work that introduces students to the step-by-step design of engineered systems and chemical processes. Courses in biotechnology, nanotechnology, medicine, law, or business may be taken as electives to give students an introduction to these applications.

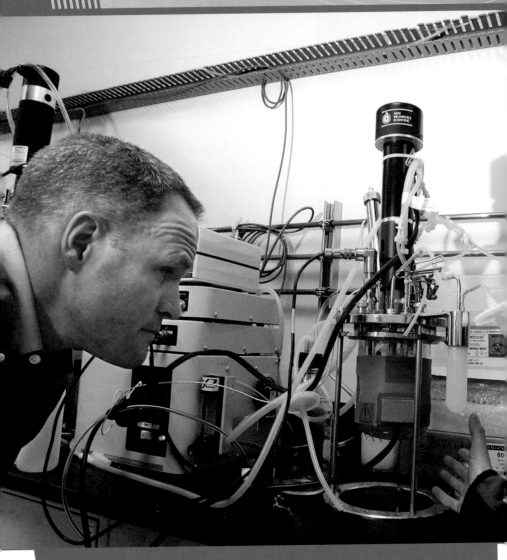

These chemical engineers are working on a $42.6 million project to develop an antimalaria drug.

Participation in the student chapter of the American Institute of Chemical Engineers (AIChE) or other engineering organizations is important. It

will give you opportunities to attend seminars and presentations given for and by chemical engineers. It will also allow you to gain a better understanding of the types of jobs that you will be qualified for upon completion of your undergraduate and graduate degrees.

Graduate Study and Licensing

Many engineers go on to pursue a master's degree. Some universities that offer a bachelor's degree offer the option of attaining a bachelor's and master's degree after five years of study. At the graduate level, students complete courses in areas such as chemical process analysis and optimization, the control of air pollution sources, polymer science, and applied mathematics in chemical engineering.

Research and publication in peer-reviewed journals is often an expected part of graduate-level study in chemical engineering. Attendance at research seminars is also expected. These requirements ensure that graduate candidates are capable

BATTERY TECHNOLOGY

The race is on for the next breakthrough in battery technology. Many companies and research institutes are working to be the first to devise an efficient and cost-effective means of extending battery life.

Whether the batteries are used for commercial and consumer applications such as toys and smart devices, or for military applications such as powering satellite telephones, a longer battery life in a more compact form is highly desirable. If batteries

Researchers at the Pacific Northwest National Laboratory display prototypes of a lithium-oxygen battery.

for large installations could last for months—or be manufactured through a process that rendered them less bulky and of lighter weight—it would be far more cost-effective to use batteries to meet the power needs of remote villages, research posts, and civilian and military ships at sea.

Chemical engineers around the world are involved in research for this new technology. The potential applications for consumer, commercial, and military applications lend a sense of urgency to their work. These engineers are often part of multidisciplinary teams investigating the possible ways that energy can be converted from one form to another for storage and later use. Some engineers are examining the potential for solar batteries. Others are dedicated to extending the capabilities of current lithium-ion batteries. In Norway, engineers are rethinking the definition and role of cathode materials in batteries. In all instances, the goal is a greener, longer-lasting battery that can be produced at a lower cost.

This type of work requires patience, attention to detail, a creative spirit, and the ability to "think outside the box" while applying mathematical and chemical principles to the problem.

of significant contributions to the field and that they are able to communicate their findings and contributions to their peers.

Although not all chemical engineers need a PE license, those with the license may have more options in terms of career advancement.

Chemical Engineers at Work

Chemical engineers work in fields that range from pharmaceuticals to waste treatment. There is a wide range of opportunities and work environments available to these professionals.

Job Opportunities

Job opportunities exist for chemical engineers in a variety of industries. There are chemical engineers at work in the petrochemical industry, in the pharmaceutical industry, and in plastic and polymer manufacturing. Chemical engineers are also employed in the food industry.

Chemical engineers work to develop new products from raw materials. They also devise new methods of converting materials into other, more useful materials. For instance, they may work on new methods for the recycling of plastics. They are an important part of teams working to produce needed materials through more efficient processes.

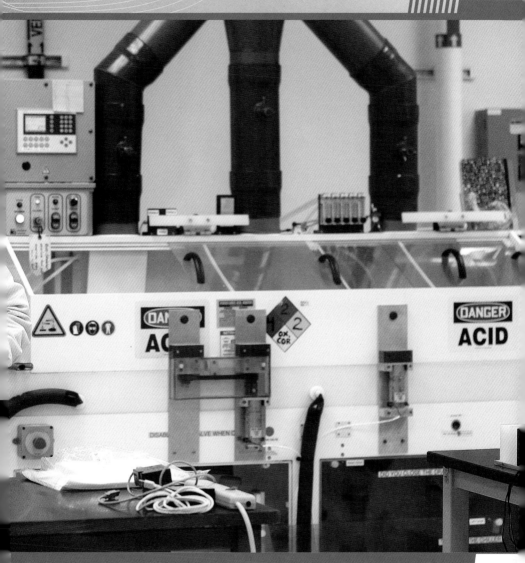

A chemical engineer changes an etching machine roller in a plant that manufactures silicon wafers for solar panels. He wears safety glasses, a lab coat, and gloves to protect against acid and other hazards.

Chemical engineers are involved in the treatment of waste materials, efforts to mitigate air and water pollution, and the production of products ranging from fertilizer to potato chips.

Workplaces

You will find chemical engineers at work in a variety of workplaces. Some are employed in labs, where they work directly with new chemicals and processes for manufacturing. Other chemical engineers focus entirely on research and development. Some of these professionals bring their own ideas to life. Others work to find ways to bring the ideas of others into widespread use.

Some chemical engineers work in medical manufacturing, creating new drugs. Others work in synthetic fiber manufacturing, creating new materials from existing and innovative processes. Still others work in chemical manufacturing.

Wherever these engineers are working, you can be sure that conditions are pristine. This is necessary in order for the results of their experimentation to be accurate. For many of the experiments performed in a chemical engineer's research, the conditions in the lab must meet exacting standards. Equipment must be calibrated properly, the temperature controlled, and specimens handled appropriately.

The employers of chemical engineers usually take safety very seriously. They have to, since many of the components these engineers work with are potentially dangerous and include materials that can become hazardous under less-than-ideal conditions.

The equipment used by these researchers is state of the art. For instance, the laboratories in use at the Worcester Polytechnic Institute in Worcester,

Massachusetts, include an Adsorption and Diffusion Laboratory for the study of the behavior of gases; a Bacterial Adhesion and Interaction Forces Laboratory for the imaging of bacteria, biopolymers, and colloidal particles; a Catalyst and Reaction Engineering Laboratory for research into fuels and chemicals from renewable resources and related studies; and a Zeolite Crystallization Laboratory for the hydrothermal synthesis of zeolites.

While the specific jobs and workplaces of chemical engineers may vary, the discipline required to envision a new process or product, design an investigation to test a new theory, and report on the findings is common to all who choose to pursue a career in this field.

CHAPTER FOUR

Civil and Environmental Engineers

C ivil engineers design and build the essential components of our infrastructure: the bridges, roads, railways, and tunnels that we rely on to get us where we're going safely. Train stations, ports, airports, parking garages, Olympic stadiums, water treatment plants, libraries, and other community buildings are also projects that call upon the expertise of civil engineers.

It is the job of the civil engineer to assess a municipality's needs now and in the future. These needs include clean water; shelter from environmental disasters such as hurricanes, tornadoes, flooding, and tsunamis; and the ability to travel from point A to point B in a timely and efficient manner. Civil engineers play an important role in meeting the needs of their communities in an intelligent and responsible manner.

Educational Requirements and Licenses

Civil engineers are called upon to keep our infrastructure up and running. To be a successful civil engineer, your coursework must include urban and rural planning, as well as advanced mathematics and engineering concepts.

High School

Successful civil engineers must have an understanding and an appreciation of urban and rural planning, engineering principles, and mathematics. To achieve this, students in high school are advised to pursue a rigorous course of study that includes upper-level mathematics and science classes. Classes that discuss how needs are assessed and resources allocated for building projects at the federal, state, and local levels are also useful. Specific science classes should include calculus and physics. AP classes in these subjects are beneficial, since they give students a clear idea of the type of material that will be covered in college.

Good communication skills are also important because many civil engineering projects involve some contact with the public. Advanced English courses can help prepare students for college coursework.

College

The courses required to earn a BS in civil engineering vary by educational institution, but it is safe to say

Sophisticated machinery such as this tunnel-boring machine is often used when working on civil engineering projects.

that any candidate for a bachelor of science degree will need to take advanced math and science courses to fulfill the major.

Statistics, Calculus III, and Differential Equations are three math courses that provide the background needed for the complex analyses that civil engineers perform. Physics, biology, and earth science classes are also on the list. These classes provide the student with a deep understanding of the forces at work in construction, as well as the impact of building projects on the ecosystem and environment.

Courses in dynamics, materials, systems, and fluid mechanics are important, too. These courses broaden candidates' outlooks while giving them the tools needed to make engineering decisions based on the materials, overall project flow, and science involved.

Thermodynamics and stress coursework is also helpful. Without an understanding of temperature and stress upon structures, it is not possible to design a robust structure that will perform well under varying conditions.

Once these requirements are met, candidates for a bachelor of science degree in civil engineering will have upper-level electives open to them. These may

Students at a girls' school observe the pressure required to break the bridge they constructed. Understanding the tolerance of materials is an important part of building structures that will meet specifications.

include courses in hydraulics, geotechnical engineering, or transportation planning and design. Taking electives in areas of interest allows students to get a taste of the work they will perform in the future. These electives

may also lead to opportunities to work on research projects with professors or as interns at local civil engineering firms.

Graduate Study and Licensing

Upon graduation with a BS in engineering, some students will undertake additional study at the graduate level. Typically, those pursuing an advanced degree in civil engineering will focus on one of four specialties. One specialty is structural engineering, or the application of engineering principles to steel and concrete bridges, buildings, and other structures. Another discipline is geotechnical engineering. Study in this area focuses on soil mechanics, engineering geology, and foundation engineering. Students may also elect to pursue additional study in the field of construction engineering and management, which covers all facets of facility planning, financing, project management, and construction. A fourth option is environmental engineering and water resources. Coursework in this area covers the related fields of hydrology, sediment

LIFE AS A CIVIL ENGINEER

In this interview, Stuart S. Nielsen, PE, tells Rosen Publishing about his career as a civil engineer. Nielsen is a methods engineer in the Office of Bridges and Structures in the Iowa Department of Transportation. He is also an adjunct faculty member at Iowa State University. His Web site, TallBridgeGuy.com, is dedicated to sustainable bridge construction.

Why did you choose a career in civil engineering?
My father is a civil engineer, and I grew up in a family construction company. I remember the pride my father had when he showed me his finished buildings, and that made a lasting impact on my life. Now I show my daughters the bridges that I have designed and the pride I have in my work.

What is your work like on a day-to-day basis?
When I was strictly a bridge designer, my primary duties were to produce bridge design plans for state projects. This would include all structural calculations to ensure the bridge was safe and met relevant design codes and a complete accounting of all the quantities (concrete, steel, etc.) necessary to build the structure.

Today, as the methods engineer, I oversee the development of statewide bridge standards, the bridge design manual, and answer structural engineering questions from our office, consultants, and county engineers.

What is the best part of being a bridge designer?
The best part for me is seeing one of my bridge designs built and knowing the secrets involved in the creation of the bridge.

Is there anything you wish you'd known in high school that would have helped you as you pursued your career?
That engineering is not exclusively math or science, that it can be a creative field and [that] engineering impacts everyone's lives.

Do you have a favorite project?
My favorite project was my design for the Keosauqua Bridge replacement. We were replacing a historic truss bridge, and we had to be very careful that our new design met the townspeople's desire for a new iconic bridge.

This project was atypical for a design engineer because it included all facets of the project. I worked with local officials and the public to develop the preliminary concept, calculated and mitigated all the hydrology concerns, and designed the final structural plans. I also worked with the contractor to construct the bridge.

transport, hydrogeology, and the effective design of containment systems.

Licensing is another important part of the qualifications for a civil engineer. Students can take the FE/EIT exam while they are seniors in college. Since there are many colleges and universities offering programs in civil engineering, the American Society of Civil Engineers (ASCE) recognized the importance of a central

This civil engineer is working on a project to repair a seawall at the Jefferson Memorial in Washington, D.C.

authority to validate the educational accomplishments of its members. With this in mind, it created the PE licensing exam. Candidates who pass this comprehensive exam have proven they are proficient in the skills

required to perform in their role as civil engineers.

Civil Engineers at Work

Civil engineers work in both the private and public sectors, in engineering and construction firms, public agencies, and government departments. The nature of the workplace depends on the specific environment that they choose for their career.

Job Opportunities

Civil engineers work for a variety of employers. Some work in the public sector, for public agencies and departments. For instance, a civil engineer might work for the county public works association or the state highway administration. Some are employees of private engineering and construction firms. Others are self-employed and work as consultants for various clients.

There are good opportunities for those with a BS in civil engineering, but many civil engineers also earn a master's degree or work to attain the designation of PE. These engineers have a wider range of engineering positions—with more advanced responsibilities and opportunities for career growth—available to them.

Workplaces

Civil engineers create infrastructure for their communities. To do this, they often need to get outside and visit sites. They also need to be inside to study topographical charts and specs. The work of a civil engineer changes from day to day. Some work is performed as part of a team, and other work is done on an individual basis. Civil engineers double-check figures. They solve the problems that arise when maintaining aging structures such as bridges and highways. Whether in the office or out in the field, at work on a team or alone, the civil engineer is focused on creating structures that will meet the needs of the community for years to come.

What Is Environmental Engineering?

Today, environmental concerns play a large part in any decision involving the use of natural resources. Will a design cause damage to the habitat of endangered animals? Will it disrupt an already fragile ecosystem? Will the resulting structure bring increased traffic to a stressed area? Will it put more strain on the available natural resources? Engineers strive to create a balance that brings a win to all the parties involved.

From such simple innovations as tunnels under roads giving turtles easier access to water, to walkways over major roadways allowing pedestrians safe passage with minimum disruption to traffic flows, environmental engineers are the professionals involved from the start. Their education and experience make them uniquely qualified to identify and assess the needs of different groups that are using the same resources. When they are able to craft a solution that gives all involved the most important parts of what they need, they have used their training, experience, and vision in a highly satisfying way.

Educational Requirements and Licenses

Environmental engineers work to keep footprints small and ecosystems healthy. To be equipped for these tasks, they must complete coursework in advanced science and mathematics.

High School

To be successful as an environmental engineer, an understanding and appreciation of chemistry, biology, physics, and engineering principles are required. Just as in preparing for a degree in civil engineering, a student who intends to pursue a degree in environmental engineering should take upper-level classes in these areas. This coursework gives students the opportunity to sample what is coming in college while demonstrating their ability to do the work. Classes such as upper-level English, in which strong communication skills can be developed and demonstrated, are also important.

College

A firm basis in engineering principles is at the heart of the environmental engineering degree. In addition to the courses required for the degree, candidates take classes that prepare them to be caretakers of the planet. Some of these classes include green building design principles, stream restoration, atmospheric chemistry, and soil biogeochemistry. Statistics, Calculus III, and Differential Equations are three classes that are part of this course of study, along with physics, biology, and earth science. The work in these classes is designed to prepare future engineers to take their knowledge and use it to protect the environment and human health.

Some undergraduate programs allow students to choose a concentration in an area of study, such as air quality, groundwater quality, or waste management.

Graduate Study and Licensing

Graduate work in environmental engineering often centers on water quality engineering. Coursework in this area includes surface and groundwater hydrology, water and wastewater treatment, waste containment and remediation, and aquatic and environmental organic chemistry. Students also study environmental law and policy.

A focus on geotechnology requires coursework in the mitigation of hazardous substances and effective methods of containment. Many programs include opportunities for graduate students to work on-site on projects that make practical use of the theories they are studying.

It is likely that any graduate program in environmental engineering will require a thorough understanding of groundwater hydrology, including the way in which the water cycle works, the effect of chemicals on the environment, and water quality control.

As is the case with other fields of engineering, the PE license for environmental engineering is recommended.

An environmental engineer pets one of two new bald eagle chicks living near a nuclear power plant in Michigan.

Environmental Engineers at Work

Environmental engineers often work on-site, where they are actively involved in reclamation projects. They also work to prepare impact statements when new projects are under consideration.

Environmental engineers are often at work on beaches and in flood regions. These engineers are responsible for reclaiming the sand washed out to sea after catastrophic storms. They work to stabilize flood plains and make it less likely that the next high-water mark will reach above the banks of the local river.

These engineers work to do more than preserve the environment. They also investigate the likelihood of seismic activity in an area slated for a new dam or bridge. They learn about the flora and fauna of an area slated for a project, too. They work to identify species that are at risk and figure out what can be done to limit the negative impact on those species.

Environmental engineering is a career in which one's passion to preserve the planet can be put to use to make a difference on a daily basis.

CHAPTER FIVE

Electrical and Computer Engineers

E lectrical engineers create technology solutions that range from handheld communication devices to face- and motion-recognition surveillance systems. Professionals in this discipline combine their deep understanding of microelectronics and power systems with creativity and innovation to produce solutions that use electrical systems to solve real-world problems.

When you use your smartphone, solve a problem with a calculator, or read the latest best seller on an e-reader, you are using a product that required the talents and vision of an electrical engineer. When you stop at a red light, get your picture snapped by a speed camera, or step into an area that is suddenly awash in light triggered by a motion sensor, you are interacting with technology that has electrical circuits and systems at its heart. This sort of technological solution is the specialty of electrical engineers.

An electrical engineer pilots his "quadcopter." The goggles allow him to see what the drone sees as it takes aerial photographs.

Educational Requirements and Licenses

Electrical engineers must have a thorough education in and understanding of advanced mathematics, physics, and mechanics. They must also be able to apply the principles of electronics to the task at hand.

High School

To prepare for a career in electrical engineering, high school students must undertake a challenging course of study. They must take upper-level mathematics and science classes, including calculus and physics at the honors and AP levels. Chemistry is also useful, as are any engineering courses offered.

Extracurricular activities in math, the sciences, engineering, and robotics will make a candidate for an engineering degree more attractive to a university. Participation in science fairs, engineering fairs, and STEM career days is also a plus.

College

Students pursuing a degree in electrical engineering complete coursework in calculus, differential equations, physics, mechanics, electrodynamics, and engineering design. They take classes in electrical circuits, discrete signal analysis, digital logic design, signal and system theory, electromagnetic

An electrical engineering major helps a middle school student solve
a problem during engineering camp at Missouri University of Science
and Technology.

theory, and electromagnetic wave propagation. These courses are necessary for a thorough understanding of the design and operation of electronic systems and circuits. Programming classes and lab work are also required.

Many undergraduate electronic engineering programs require the completion of a culminating project during the senior year. The purpose of the project is to demonstrate the student's ability to create and implement a successful design. The specifics of the project vary with the individual student's interests.

Electrical engineering majors may elect to specialize in computer engineering, controls, electrophysics, microelectronics, power systems, or other related areas.

Graduate Study and Licensing

Many electrical engineering students elect to complete a master's degree in electrical engineering. This degree focuses on research in a number of areas, including communications and networking; control, robotics, and dynamical systems; circuits and systems; and applied electromagnetics. Many of these research areas and projects are multidisciplinary, bringing the student into contact with team members from various disciplines, including physical science and technology, nanophysics, and advanced materials. The goal of these research teams is to produce components that use energy more efficiently, work at higher speeds than existing components, and are smaller and more compact than the current technology. These improvements are desired because they will lead to lower-cost, higher-performance devices.

Those seeking the PE designation can participate in the licensing process. There is a PE exam specifically for electrical and electronics specialties, as well as for power specialties.

Electrical Engineers at Work

Electrical engineers have careers in fields ranging from robotics to nanotechnology. Their skills are in demand in a variety of workplaces.

Job Opportunities

Electrical engineers are sought after for a range of careers. They hold positions in robotics, the design of controls and communications systems for medical applications, and the design of electronic components for a vast array of technology products. Electrical engineers are also needed to develop

This electrical engineer works on a project to build and assemble equipment for a deep-sea observatory in the Pacific Ocean. The titanium cylinders will house scientific instruments underwater.

improvements in wind, solar, and traditional energy systems and power sources for electric-powered vehicles.

NANOTECHNOLOGY

When people speak about the history of nanotechnology, they often mention Richard Feynman. Feynman was an American theoretical physicist and Nobel Prize winner. His talk, "There's Plenty of Room at the Bottom," was presented at the annual meeting of the American Physical Society at Caltech on December 29, 1959.

A research engineer handles silicon wafers in a diffusion furnace. The research is being conducted at the Nanotechnology Research and Education Center at the University of South Florida.

In his talk, Feynman invited those in attendance to imagine what would happen if they could directly manipulate atoms: "Consider, for example, a piece of material in which we make little coils and condensers (or their solid state analogs) 1,000 or 10,000 angstroms in a circuit, one right next to the other, over a large area, with little antennas sticking out at the other end—a whole series of circuits. Is it possible, for example, to emit light from a whole set of antennas, like we emit radio waves from an organized set of antennas to beam the radio programs to Europe? The same thing would be to beam the light out in a definite direction with very high intensity."

Because of Feynman's reputation, his remarks had a great impact on the scientists of his time and those who followed. His influence was felt in the drive to create an apparatus that would allow the study of matter at smaller and smaller sizes.

Today, electrical and computer engineers are working with ever-smaller components. Computers that once took up an entire room now sit atop a desk—or fit inside a pocket. How small can these components get? Engineers are just beginning to tap the full potential of nanotechnology. Just how small they can realistically go remains to be seen, but it is known that for every significant reduction in the size of computer chips and other components, there is a corresponding increase in performance and a reduction in manufacturing costs. Anxious to benefit from these advances, companies and governments are looking to electrical and computer engineers to translate them into practical technologies.

Workplaces

Most electrical engineers work in a lab or industrial plant, where they supervise computer programmers, electricians, scientists, and other engineers. The lab environment for an electrical engineer must be pristine to ensure that any components are free from the smallest particles of foreign matter.

The individual workspace of an electrical engineer varies with the role played on a particular job. An engineer might work in a lab for part of the day and in an office for the rest of that day. Often, an electrical engineer draws upon communication skills in a team effort to develop a new device.

What Is Computer Engineering?

Computer engineers apply the principles and techniques of a variety of disciplines, including electrical engineering, computer science, and mathematical analysis, to the design of computer software and hardware systems. They also develop, test, and evaluate the systems they design to ensure that the designs result in enhanced performance.

When you make a deposit at an ATM, swipe your debit card at the point of purchase, place an online order, or speak to the navigation system in your car, you are interacting with technology that was designed, developed, tested, and perfected by computer engineers. When you interact with a computerized device by means of a touch pad, mouse, stylus, or virtual buttons, you are enjoying the versatility that comes from a robust computer interface. This is also the result of the work done by talented and creative computer engineers.

Educational Requirements and Licenses

Computer engineers design the "guts" of a computer. As a result, computer engineering requires a thorough knowledge of mathematics and electric circuits.

High School

Preparation for a degree in computer engineering begins in high school. It is best to take four years of math, including calculus. Computer programming classes are also advised. Science coursework is important, including classes at the AP level.

Participation in extracurricular clubs and activities that focus on the skills required for success in computer engineering is a definite plus. Work with your guidance office to bring speakers and programs to your school if none are currently offered. Take the time to explore the resources available to you through the IEEE, the professional organization for electrical and computer engineers.

College, Graduate School, and Licensing

The courses required for a bachelor's degree in computer engineering include calculus, differential equations, discrete structures, physics, mechanics, and vibrations. There is also required coursework in electric circuits, discrete signal analysis, digital logic design, and analog and digital electronics. Classes in computer systems and the organization of programming languages, object-oriented programming, algorithms, and operating systems are also required.

To earn a master's degree, additional courses and research in computer engineering; circuits and systems; control, robotics, and dynamical systems; communications and networking; and related disciplines are required.

The PE license is also suggested for computer engineering professionals. The licensing process is the same as for other engineering fields. There is a specific exam for those seeking the PE designation in computer engineering.

Computer Engineers at Work

Computer engineers have a range of opportunities available to them. They often use their skills on the design side at labs and high-tech manufacturing companies.

Job Opportunities

Computer engineers are employed to design robots, develop microprocessors, and design supercomputers and smart devices. They develop programs for advanced computer applications and create integrated

An associate professor at the School of Electrical and Computer Engineering at Georgia Tech works on the SnoMate robot. The robot is designed to gather scientific data in icy conditions.

circuits for semiconductor fabrication. They create not only security and cryptographic systems, but also software systems and network protocols.

You will find computer engineers employed in the fields of artificial intelligence, computer design, software engineering, computer theory, and operating systems and network development. Their roles range from hands-on researchers to team leaders and supervisors of other engineering professionals.

Computer engineers are sought after in these fields because of their understanding of computer systems and computer technology. These engineers are familiar with computers from the circuits (hardware) to the operating system (software). Often, they are instrumental in the development of new programming paradigms. Their ability to envision a problem in a new way is integral to their effectiveness as researchers and applied professionals.

As more and more tasks are performed by computerized systems, the talents of experienced computer engineers will continue to be valued.

Workplaces

You will find many computer engineers at work in research laboratories, where they build and test a variety of computer models. Some of the research laboratories are affiliated with high-tech manufacturing companies. Labs of research and development firms and the federal government employ other computer engineers. Firms located in metropolitan areas provide the most opportunities.

Both electrical and computer engineers are in demand because of the growing use of computers and smart devices, from cell phones and tablets to Bluetooth-enabled watches and cameras. As the demand for these products continues to grow, there will be a greater market for more powerful and efficient versions, as well as completely new items. Electrical and computer engineers are the professionals with the education and experience to design, test, and implement these innovations and improvements.

CHAPTER SIX

Mechanical Engineers

Mechanical engineers are engineers who build things. From packaging to zippers, door hinges to deadbolt locks, mechanical engineers work on the products and devices that we use and interact with every day. These devices include simple things like pens and tools. They also include more complex items, such as lunar rovers and solar panels. The one thing they all have in common is that someone—a mechanical engineer—worked with a variety of materials and technologies to create a solution to an engineering problem.

Mechanical engineers designed the heating and cooling system components at work in your home. The cooling system at the ice rink, the irrigation systems in the school garden, the braking and exhaust systems in the family car—all are systems that required the work of a mechanical engineer at some point in the design cycle.

Educational Requirements and Licenses

Mechanical engineers must be able to combine their technical knowledge of engineering with practical considerations. Courses in mathematics, science, fluid dynamics, and the manufacturing process are just part of the requirements for careers in this field.

High School

If your heart is set on a career as a mechanical engineer, you have probably been tinkering with things all your life. In high school, you can begin the formal study required for this degree. Be sure to take classes in physics, geometry, algebra, calculus, statistics, and engineering. Advanced classes are a must, so include AP calculus and physics if possible. To demonstrate your strong communication skills, include honors or AP English, too.

Make the time to participate in extracurricular activities and clubs with a focus on topics related to engineering. Robotics clubs and competitions, science fair projects, guest lectures by visiting scientists and engineers—all of these will help prepare you for the work that you will be required to do in college. These activities and experiences will also help you gain entry into a mechanical engineering program.

College

Those pursuing a bachelor's degree in mechanical engineering complete coursework in mechanics, dynamics, thermodynamics, and fluid mechanics. They also complete a series of classes in computer-aided design and product engineering and manufacturing.

A mechanical engineering major enjoys a ride in the lightweight car he designed and constructed. In the future, he would like to see the vehicle used in developing countries.

An understanding of vibration, control, and optimization, along with coursework in engineering materials and the manufacturing process, is also required to prepare students to design and develop mechanical devices.

Some elective classes that may be offered include robotics for medical and other applications, fiber optics, manufacturing automation, and quality control in the production process. Familiarity with a variety of tools and instruments is also required.

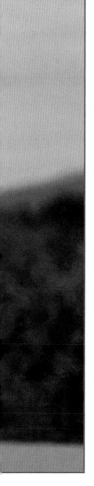

Participation in the student chapter of the American Society of Mechanical Engineers (ASME) is recommended. This organization provides students with opportunities to network, find mentors and internships, and prepare for the exams that lead to the PE license.

Graduate Study and Licensing

Candidates for a master's degree in mechanical engineering take courses that prepare them for work in engineering design. These classes include engineering design methods, decision making, and optimization. Many students also take advanced courses in mechanics, materials and thermodynamics, and failure mechanisms and reliability.

Advanced mathematics courses are also part of the graduate coursework. These classes cover topics including differential geometry, chaos theory, stochastic process, sampling theory, and regression and analysis of variance. Some of the material in these classes comes into play during the design phase. Other material equips the student with the tools needed to assess manufacturing performance once a product is in production.

Those holding a degree in mechanical engineering will want to attain the PE license for the mechanical engineering specialty most closely aligned with their future career.

Mechanical Engineers at Work

Mechanical engineers make things happen. They use their technical knowledge and imagination to solve problems. Their skills are in demand in a wide variety of fields and workplaces.

Job Opportunities

Job opportunities for mechanical engineers are plentiful. Their skills are needed anywhere the principles of science and mathematics are used to develop economical solutions to technical problems. You will find mechanical engineers at work interpreting

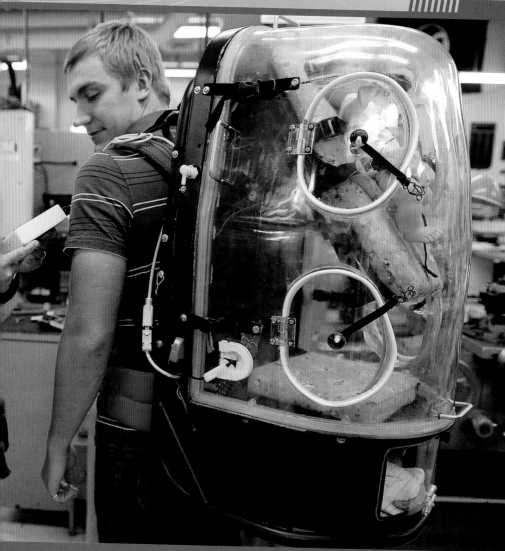

Mechanical engineers work to solve technical problems. This professor and graduate student assess the performance of a medically equipped, portable incubator to transport infants in undeveloped areas.

blueprints and schematics, analyzing design proposals, and producing product specifications. They work to resolve system malfunctions, and they

WOMEN IN ENGINEERING

For much of history, careers in science, technology, engineering, and mathematics were seen as ones with unlimited opportunity for men and virtually no opportunity for women. There were very few female doctors and even fewer female engineers. History books are filled with the accomplishments of male engineers during the Industrial Revolution and in the decades since. It was assumed that women were better in the "softer" disciplines, such as English, history, and education. Mathematics and science were seen as tailor-made for men.

Careers in engineering are open to both men and women. All that is needed is adequate preparation, a willingness to work with others, and a curious and innovative mind.

All of this has changed in recent years. There are now women in every branch of engineering. Girls are being encouraged to pursue a STEM course load in high school and college. There are also organizations and initiatives designed to encourage girls to pursue careers in engineering. Engineer Girl is an organization that supports and promotes STEM careers for girls from high school onward. Part of the National Academy of Engineering, the Engineer Girl Web site (http://www.engineergirl.org) offers information, interviews, and ways for girls to get involved in engineering fields. The site lists competitions and contests, information about engineering organizations and scholarships, and steps that girls can take while still in high school.

The IEEE has established IEEE Women in Engineering (WIE), the largest international professional organization dedicated to promoting women in the STEM fields and encouraging girls to pursue engineering careers. There are WIE chapters at colleges and universities around the world. They offer programs and opportunities for women pursuing degrees in engineering.

The result of these efforts is the realization and celebration that engineering is not about gender. It is about the way an individual—male or female—defines a problem and uses the tools at hand to craft a solution. The qualities it takes to be a successful engineer—a strong work ethic, an interest and aptitude in the STEM subjects, and the ability to imagine new solutions to existing problems—are ones that both men and women possess.

A mechanical engineer rides the prize-winning Aquaduct Concept Vehicle by IDEO. Intended for use in developing nations, the three-wheel cycle filters dirty water into drinking water as the rider pedals.

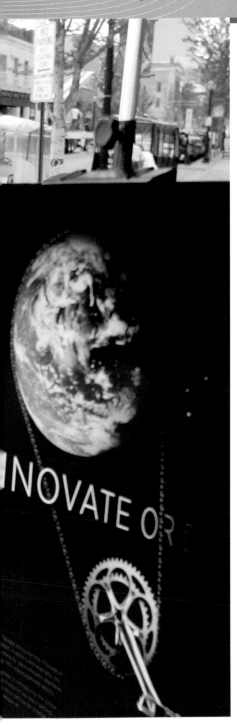

research and trouble-shoot mechanical failures in a variety of situations.

There is a need for mechanical engineers in factories and production facilities. Their talents are needed to ensure that the resulting products meet specifications, the processes are carried out in the most cost-effective way, and the proper equipment is used for the job.

You will also find mechanical engineers in the field. They may be overseeing the installation of a special-purpose piece of machinery. They may be on a sales call with a potential customer who wants information about the specifications and tolerances for a piece of equipment. They may be meeting with a client to learn more about the client's requirements for a new piece of equipment. Later, they can decide if existing equipment can be

A mechanical engineer at the National Wind Technology Center evaluates a prototype blade for wind turbines. Tests will be conducted to determine the strengths and weaknesses of the materials used in the construction of the blade.

modified to meet the need or a new design would be more cost effective.

Mechanical engineers are involved in the design and implementation of machinery and equipment for dams and other power sources. They are at work wherever control apparatuses and equipment are designed and tested.

Mechanical engineers also work in supervisory capacities, overseeing production works, technicians, designs, and safety procedures. They are often involved in the application of engineering principles and practices to emerging fields, such as biomedical engineering.

Workplaces

Mechanical engineers work in diverse settings. They are employed in factories and other production facilities. They are also employed in corporate environments, where they are involved in the design of production facilities and production lines. You may find mechanical engineers at work at construction sites or in research facilities, where teams of engineers pool their expertise as they tackle an important problem.

Because there are so many options available to mechanical engineers, it is possible to find a work environment that suits your interests and preferences. If mechanical equipment is your focus, you might choose to work at a manufacturing facility. There, you may be close to the equipment you've designed and to the components you've brought from design to production. If power generation is your focus, you might choose to work in the field, overseeing the installation of electric generators, internal combustion engines, and steam and gas turbines.

A wide range of opportunities is open to those with degrees in mechanical engineering. This provides the engineer with some choice in terms of work function and workplace. Be sure to consider your talents and interests when deciding where to put your focus. Then enjoy the flexibility you have as a result of your hard work.

CHAPTER SEVEN

Job Search Basics

It may sound like silly advice, but the best time to prepare for a job search is before you need a job. Think about it. When you graduate from college or from graduate school, if you haven't done the groundwork necessary to get your first job, it's a bit late in the game to start. You can, of course, go into high gear and prepare the materials you'll need. How much better would it be to take a reasoned approach to your job search? The ideas below help ensure your time pursuing an engineering position will be used to your best possible advantage.

Plan Ahead

If you have your heart set on a career in engineering, chances are good that you've been looking for opportunities to give it a try for as long as you can remember. Perhaps you've been part of a robotics club at your elementary school. Maybe you've taken part in a competition or showcase at your middle school. If you have, you are likely to have earned a certificate for your participation—or maybe even a prize for one of your designs.

From reading this and other resources, you are well aware of the rigorous requirements for entry into a college engineering program. You know that you must take advanced-level courses in mathematics and science. You also know that your participation in extracurricular activities, science fairs, and volunteer work or internships will be of interest to those considering your application into an engineering program.

It can be helpful to work with a peer when preparing your résumé or application.

You may think you will always remember the details of the clubs you belonged to and the activities you enjoyed, but that is not necessarily the case. Taking the time now to create a portfolio with a recap of your activities will save you a lot of time when you apply to undergraduate and graduate programs and apply for your first job.

Your Résumé and Cover Letter

The first thing you will need to do is prepare a résumé and cover letter. The résumé lists your relevant experience. It includes the degrees you've earned, research you've conducted, articles you've published, and any clubs or activities you've been involved in. You can use your portfolio to jog your memory and make certain that you include all the relevant experience and information.

Be sure to look at some samples when preparing your résumé. There are many books with examples of résumés. The career center at your college should have resources available, such as sample résumés, résumé workshops, and review services. Some engineering organizations provide résumé templates, too. Give yourself enough time to set the document aside for a few days before coming back to it for the final review.

A cover letter is another vital part of the job search. Most cover letters follow the same general format. However, each letter is geared to portray your qualifications for a specific position or position within a certain company. You can find samples of cover letters from a variety of sources. The goal is to craft a letter that is polite and formal yet natural. Imagine you are speaking directly to the person who has opened your letter and is about to decide whether to set your letter aside or pass it along for further consideration. What would you say to that person? Your cover letter is your chance.

Contacts

As was the case with your extracurricular activities and engineering-related experiences, you have been building a list of contacts throughout your academic career. You never know who might help you land your first job. It could be a favorite engineering teacher from high school. It could be the mentor you had during a summer internship or the professor who first hired you as a research assistant. If you've been participating in the full range of opportunities available to you as you have completed your schooling, you will likely have contacts who are willing to help you in your job search.

Your participation in the student chapter of engineering associations is another way that you can make contacts. You can meet professional engineers by attending presentations. You can read the work of researchers whom you admire and contact them about their work. You can volunteer for committees and other groups that are involved in engineering programs and activities. If you enjoy these opportunities and take the time to get to know the people you meet, these people are more likely to make themselves available to you as you begin your job search.

Job Search Skills

Getting your first job can be difficult. You don't have a lot of real-world experience. How could you? You are

Job fairs are an excellent opportunity to learn about different organizations and the opportunities they offer.

YOUR PORTFOLIO

Taking the time to create a portfolio makes a lot of sense for an aspiring engineer. All of the information you need for applying to jobs and schools will be in

Were you an intern during the summer? Be sure to include documentation of your work in your portfolio. This engineering student created an app to control a Mars rover at NASA's Jet Propulsion Laboratory.

one place. There's no need for you to share your portfolio with anyone else. This type of portfolio is primarily for your use. It's designed to have the information you need in a format that makes it easy to compile a résumé or complete a job application. Why not include the following in your portfolio?

- A form for each activity that includes the name of the club or activity, the dates you were involved in that activity, the nature of the activity, the name and contact information for any advisors or mentors, letters of recommendation from those same advisors and mentors, and a brief recap of your experience
- Awards, certificates, or other forms of recognition for your work and participation
- Photos, posters, and presentation materials that were produced while you were involved in the activity
- Copies of college essays and job applications that you have prepared

While you are creating this portfolio primarily to simplify your life when preparing a résumé or completing an application, there may be times when it is appropriate to share parts of or your entire portfolio with a prospective employer or mentor. Be selective, choosing materials that relate to that specific person or company.

familiar with the latest research and techniques in your field, however. This is of value to a potential employer. You also have a list of accomplishments that you can use to demonstrate your abilities.

Common job-search strategies are to look for a job online or go to a headhunter—an employment recruiter who will help you find a job. Another excellent opportunity is to attend the job fairs held at your college. During these job fairs, representatives from a variety of companies will come to conduct interviews on campus. Bring your résumé, as you may have the opportunity to meet with a recruiter. These opportunities are often announced in advance so that you have the chance to sign up and prepare.

The Interview

Whether your initial interview is in the form of a meeting on campus or in the offices of the firm that you hope will hire you, remember that there are important rules that apply.

First, you need to dress in a way that indicates you take the opportunity seriously and are capable of conducting yourself in a professional manner. Ask the career center what the typical dress code is for recruiter visits to campus. It may not be as formal as a suit and tie, but it is surely not as casual as basketball shorts and a crop top. When visiting the offices of an engineering firm or laboratory, dress slacks or a skirt, a dress shirt, and a sports jacket or blazer are all

Dress appropriately for an interview. Make eye contact. Shake hands with a firm grip. Turn negatives into positives by explaining what you learned from any less-than-optimal experiences.

appropriate choices. A tie for men and dress shoes for men and women are also called for.

Be sure to arrive a bit before your meeting time. This will give you a chance to catch your breath and prepare yourself for the interview. You'll also have time to complete any forms that may be required. Take the time that you have to review your engineering-related accomplishments. Be prepared to answer the questions asked, turning any negatives into positives and including your qualifications for the job whenever possible.

Make eye contact. Shake hands with a firm grip. Listen to the question being asked, rather than focusing on what you are going to say. Be prepared with questions of your own—questions about career advancement, for instance.

Don't be afraid to ask for the job. Make it clear that you have looked at a number of possible positions and this one especially interests you. State several reasons why. You may not get the job, but it won't be because they didn't realize you wanted it.

Follow Up

If possible, get a business card from the person who interviews you. This will have the information you need for the thank-you note you will write to the interviewer. Thank the person for the opportunity to speak to him or her about the position. Mention again some of the reasons why you are a good fit for the position and say that you hope to hear from him or her soon.

If you don't get a business card, don't worry. Remember the name of the person interviewing you. You can call and ask the receptionist or administrative assistant for the information you need the next day. Be sure to follow up within a few days of your interview.

When it is time to search for your next position, it won't be as difficult. You'll not only have the experience of finding and landing this first job, but you'll also have the work experience and credentials that come from your first position. You'll also have a good feel for the type of work you want to do next, along with valuable contacts you've made. All in all, you'll be in a position to reflect on this first job search and use what worked, combined with new job-hunting strategies you've discovered.

CHAPTER EIGHT

Staying Current

For engineers, the current state of knowledge is constantly in flux. Each new research project, theory, or application of existing technology pushes the boundaries of what was known previously. Each new use of technology, new process, or new discovery adds another layer to the knowledge base shared by all engineers. For engineers to be at the top of their game, it's necessary for them to be aware of new breakthroughs and new uses for existing technology.

Organizations

Many engineers stay informed through their membership in professional associations. In addition to general engineering associations and societies, there are organizations for each specialty in engineering. These sponsor programs, workshops, and annual meetings that include presentations

The 2011 IEEE International Conference in Robotics and Automation was held in Shanghai, China. The theme of the conference was "Better Robots, Better Life."

by researchers and professionals who are prominent in their fields.

By belonging to these organizations and attending these functions, engineers can keep abreast of

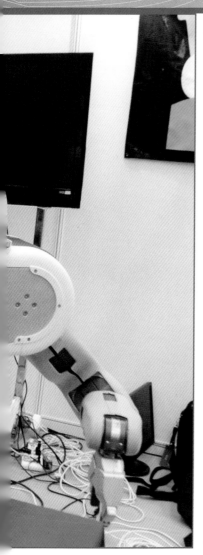

new information while meeting with colleagues from across the country and around the world. The personal relationships that are forged allow for the informal transmission of knowledge as well. In addition, many organizations offer classes and training in areas of interest to those working in a particular specialty.

Committees

Many organizations have committees that oversee curriculum development or plan and run the annual meeting. Professionals who volunteer to help in these capacities work with others who share similar interests. They identify and recruit speakers and review proposals for panels and lectures, learning about the newest trends and developments in the process.

Some committees work with undergraduate and graduate students as they pursue their engineering degrees. These positions are perfect for professionals who want to share their enthusiasm for engineering with those just getting started in the field. As they review student presentations, these engineers are keeping tabs on the latest findings.

THE ABC'S OF PROFESSIONAL ASSOCIATIONS

AAES. IEEE. WIE. ASCE. NCEES. It may seem like alphabet soup, but each of these acronyms stands for a well-respected engineering organization.

You will learn more about these organizations as you pursue your BS degree because nearly all of them

Concrete canoes? Why not? Each year at the National Concrete Canoe Competition of the American Society of Civil Engineers (ASCE), teams from engineering schools meet to compete.

have student chapters at schools with accredited engineering programs. These chapters offer support, programs, and information that will be invaluable to you as you complete your coursework. They also will provide opportunities to attend lectures and other programs that will be of interest to you.

You can learn more about these organizations while you are still in school. One simple way to do this is to visit the Web site for the American Association of Engineering Societies (AAES), at http://www.aaes .org. The resources section of this site includes videos from different specialty engineering societies. You can also contact the AAES for information on engineering societies for your particular specialty.

Finally, you can contact the specialized engineering department at your local university. Ask which organizations provide support and information for engineers in that field. Once you have the names, be sure to take some time to become familiar with the resources and materials available to you.

Professional associations can play a vital role in your continuing education over the life of your engineering career. These associations hold annual seminars, programs on special topics, and workshops. They provide the chance to interact with other engineering professionals to network and learn about job opportunities and research projects that are under way.

Taking the time to be active in your professional association will provide you with opportunities for continued education and the chance to interact with other professionals who share your interests.

Journals

Quite often, membership in a professional organization includes a subscription to one of the many journals published by the organization. The journals

Journals, lectures, seminars, and classes offer a way for practicing engineers to stay current on the latest research.

offer papers and articles by those who are making advances in the field. By reading the journals, engineering professionals can learn about the newest innovations, designs, and projects. There is information about new equipment and processes as well. Journal articles often include information about the authors, allowing other engineers to contact these individuals to discuss their work.

Lectures, Classes, and Seminars

Lectures at universities are often open to the public. By attending these lectures, engineering professionals are able to keep on top of the latest information. Some firms and research facilities bring in researchers from other fields to present information on their work. The hope is that by making their employees familiar with work in related fields, they will spur their workers to look at the problems that they are trying to solve in a new light.

Engineers can also take classes at their local university as a way of keeping up with new technologies. For example, as research in nanotechnology makes advances, classes on nanotechnology offer a way for engineers to cover the basics quickly and thoroughly.

Many colleges offer seminars on topics such as nanobiology, chemical containment, and advances in robotics. For engineering professionals, these seminars are opportunities for education and networking. There is often time to interact with the people making the presentations. During these interactions, connections that may lead to further educational opportunities are often made.

ENGINEERS WITHOUT BORDERS

People in developing countries face challenges that may seem incredible to those who live in countries with a dependable infrastructure. For the people in these struggling communities, clean water, reliable power sources, and roads that are passable in good weather and bad are necessities they may go without.

In 2000, Bernard Amadei, professor of civil engineering at the University of Colorado at Boulder, met Angel Tzec, a landscaper and representative of the Belize Ministry of Agriculture. The two men became friends, and Tzec invited Dr. Amadei to visit his village.

Engineers Without Borders brings engineers, engineering students, and local communities in need together to solve an engineering problem, such as improving drinking water safety.

The village had no running water, electricity, or sanitation. Dr. Amadei was shocked to see young children at work, carrying water to the village from a nearby river, all day long. As a civil engineer, he knew there had to be something he could do to change the situation.

Amadei brought a team of eight University of Colorado-Boulder students, along with civil engineering expert Denis Walsh, to solve the problem. By working with the community, they were able to use an existing waterfall to create a clean water system. The cost was nominal. The time it took was short. The solution was tailor-made and solved the specific problem.

Dr. Amadei realized that professional and student engineers could help with similar problems on a global basis. These small project teams could work at the local level to bring about needed change without the involvement of larger government entities. As a result, they could complete the projects for far less money and in far less time.

In 2002, Dr. Amadei founded Engineers Without Borders USA. The model is simple: projects are submitted for consideration. All that's needed is a partnering organization in the local community. Engineers and engineering students from an EWB-USA chapter then strategize to meet the need in an effective and efficient manner.

EWB-USA provides a forum for engineers and engineering students to have a real and immediate impact on the lives of people who would otherwise have no other source of help. Today, there are more than twelve thousand students, faculty, and engineering professionals working to complete urgently needed projects involving sanitation, agriculture, civil works, energy, information systems, and water supplies.

A poster session is often part of a class or seminar. During these sessions, researchers present their findings in the form of elaborate posters. The researchers are available for questions and discussion. These poster sessions are a perfect way for engineers to learn about the cutting-edge research being performed in a given engineering field.

Mentorship and Recruiting

Engineering professionals can serve as mentors and college recruiters. As mentors, they work with young

Workshops often include a hands-on component in which experienced engineers assess the work produced by workshop participants.

professionals or interns as they adjust to life as an engineer. Some young people may be "trying on" the field for the summer or beginning the first job of their career. Whatever the case, the mentor meets with the individuals and helps them find their place in the company and the field. As they work with these young engineers, opportunities arise to discuss the engineering work that is being done.

Meeting with applicants for college engineering programs is another way that engineers can stay abreast of changes in engineering technology. As part of the recruitment process, engineers must be prepared to answer—and ask—questions about the current state of the field. Doing so through the process of recruiting students for an engineering program can be informative and enjoyable.

Volunteering

Very often, engineering professionals find that their skills and experience are of great value to high schools and school boards. Some professionals work with engineering clubs at the high school level, introducing students to the latest thinking in their field. Volunteers can also serve as advisors on curriculum panels and in the selection of textbooks for classes in the STEM fields. The knowledge these professionals have attained over the course of their careers, supplemented by the new information that they have acquired by reading journals and attending conferences, results in constant demand for their expertise, even after retirement.

Lifelong Learning

Whichever engineering discipline one selects, it is important to understand that a career in engineering requires the engineer to be a lifelong learner. There will always be a new technology on the horizon. New applications for existing technology will continue to evolve. New problems that urgently need solutions will inevitably arise. These developments present an opportunity for a curious mind to be engaged in learning for years after the initial degree requirements are met.

For those with a passion for applying science and technology to the pressing problems of today, a career in engineering is an invitation to a lifetime of discovery.

GLOSSARY

ARTIFICIAL INTELLIGENCE A branch of computer science that gives systems the ability to respond to their environment in a way that imitates intelligent human behavior.

ELECTIVE A course that can be taken after the core required courses are completed.

GRANT Monies awarded to those who meet certain criteria.

INTERNSHIP An opportunity to work, often without pay, for the purpose of gaining experience.

LICENSE Proof that an individual has attained a certain level of proficiency as a professional.

MITIGATION The process of making something less severe or harmful.

MUNICIPALITY A city, town, or other area with a clear boundary and form of government.

NANOMATERIAL A chemical substance or material that is manufactured and used on a very small scale. It is measured in nanometers (one-billionth of a meter).

NATURAL RESOURCE A material that occurs in nature and has economic value.

PEER-REVIEWED Checked by experts in the field who are qualified to judge the merit of a scholarly work.

PORTFOLIO An organized collection of materials that represents a person's best work.

RECLAMATION The process of protecting, restoring, and improving land.

RESERVOIR An area where water pools and is stored, usually behind a dam or other barrier.

REVOLUTIONIZE To cause a change in the way something is performed or perceived.

RIGOROUS Difficult, exacting, and challenging.

ROBOTICS A technology that deals with the design and development of robots and the software that controls them.

SCHOLARSHIP Money that is awarded for education-related expenses.

SEISMIC Related or pertaining to the vibration of the earth.

SKILL SET The skills with which a person is proficient, usually developed through training and/or experience.

STEM Acronym for the fields of science, technology, engineering, and mathematics.

SUSTAINABLE Involving methods that do not use up valuable or scarce natural resources.

TUITION The amount that a college charges for instruction.

WORK-STUDY PROGRAM An arrangement with a college in which a student works on campus to make money to pay for tuition and expenses.

FOR MORE INFORMATION

American Society of Civil Engineers (ASCE)
1801 Alexander Bell Drive
Reston, VA 20191
(800) 548-2723
Web site: http://www.asce.org
The ASCE provides a strong base of support for the civil engineering community. It offers resources for employers, students, faculty, children, parents, and teachers.

American Society of Mechanical Engineers (ASME)
1828 L Street NW, #906
Washington, DC 20036
(202) 785-3756
Web site: http://www.asme.org
The ASME enables career enrichment, skills development, collaboration, and knowledge sharing across all engineering disciplines. It serves a diverse membership, from college students and early-career engineers to project managers, corporate executives, researchers, and academic leaders.

Biomedical Engineering Society (BMES)
8201 Corporate Drive, Suite 1125
Landover, MD 20785-2224
(301) 459-1999
Web site: http://www.bmes.org
The BMES is a society of professionals devoted to developing and using engineering and technology to advance human health and well-being.

Canadian Medical and Biological Engineering Society (CMBES)
CMBES Secretariat
1485 Laperriere Avenue
Ottawa, ON K1Z 7S8
Canada
(613) 728-1759
Web site: http://www.cmbes.ca
The CMBES is Canada's principal society for medical and biological engineering. It works to advance the theory and practice of medical device technology and serves as a forum for information exchange among health care professionals, scientists, and the general public.

Canadian Society for Civil Engineering (CSCE)
4877 Sherbrooke Street West
Montreal, QC H3Z 1G9
Canada
(514) 933-2634
Web site: http://www.csce.ca
The CSCE works to develop and maintain high standards of civil engineering practice in Canada and enhance the public image of the civil engineering profession.

National Science Foundation (NSF)
4201 Wilson Boulevard
Arlington, VA 22230
(703) 292-5111

Web site: http://www.nsf.gov

The NSF is a federal agency whose mission includes support for all fields of fundamental science and engineering, except for the medical sciences. It ensures that research is fully integrated with education so that the new discoveries of today are used to train the scientists and engineers of tomorrow.

National Society of Professional Engineers (NSPE)
1420 King Street
Alexandria, VA 22314
(703) 684-2800
Web site: http://www.nspe.org

This is an organization of licensed professional engineers (PEs) and engineer interns (EIs). It offers education, licensure advocacy, leadership training, and networking to its members while enhancing their ability to ethically and professionally practice engineering.

Society for Science & the Public
1719 N Street NW
Washington, DC 20036
(202) 785-2255
Web site: https://www.societyforscience.org

The Society for Science & the Public is dedicated to public engagement in scientific research and education. It offers science news for students and links to its special programs implemented with corporate support, including the Intel International Science and Engineering Fair and the Intel Science Talent Search.

Society of Women Engineers (SWE)
203 N. La Salle Street, Suite 1675
Chicago, IL 60601
(877) 793-4636
Web site: http://societyofwomenengineers.swe.org
The SWE is the oldest society dedicated to the advancement of women in engineering. It works to stimulate women to achieve their full potential in careers as engineers and leaders, expand the image of the engineering profession as a positive force in society, and demonstrate the value of diversity.

Web Sites

Due to the changing nature of Internet links, Rosen Publishing has developed an online list of Web sites related to the subject of this book. This site is updated regularly. Please use this link to access the list:

http://www.rosenlinks.com/STEM/Eng

FOR FURTHER READING

Agardy, Franklin J., and Patrick J. Sullivan. *Environmental Engineering: Environmental Health and Safety for Municipal Infrastructure, Land Use & Planning, and Industry.* Hoboken, NJ: Wiley, 2009.

Baine, Celeste. *Is There an Engineer Inside You? A Comprehensive Guide to Career Decisions in Engineering.* Eugene, OR: Engineering Education Service Center, 2013.

Brockman, Reed, and Celeste Baine. *From Sundaes to Space Stations: Careers in Civil Engineering.* Seattle, WA: Engineering Education Service Center, 2011.

Cantú, Norma Elia. *Paths to Discovery: Autobiographies from Chicanas with Careers in Science, Mathematics, and Engineering.* Los Angeles, CA: UCLA Chicano Studies Research Center Press, 2008.

Farr, J. Michael. *Top 100 Computer and Technical Careers: Your Complete Guidebook to Major Jobs in Many Fields at All Training Levels.* Indianapolis, IN: JIST Publishing, 2009.

Freeman, Richard B., and Daniel L. Goroff. *Science and Engineering Careers in the United States: An Analysis of Markets and Employment.* Chicago, IL: University of Chicago Press, 2009.

Frize, Monique, Peter R. D. Frize, and Nadine Faulkner. *The Bold and the Brave: A History of Women in Science and Engineering.* Ottawa, ON, Canada: University of Ottawa Press, 2009.

Graedel, T. E., and Braden R. Allenby. *Industrial Ecology and Sustainable Engineering.* Upper Saddle River, NJ: Prentice Hall, 2010.

Institute for Career Research. *Careers in Electrical Engineering: Electronics Engineer.* Chicago, IL: Institute for Career Research, 2012.

Institute for Career Research. *Careers in Engineering: Structural Engineer.* Chicago, IL: Institute for Research, 2008.

Institute for Career Research. *Careers in Robotics.* Chicago, IL: Institute for Career Research, 2012.

Institute for Career Research. *Engineering and Technical Careers in Green Energy.* Chicago, IL: Institute for Career Research, 2011.

JIST Works. *STEM Careers: Guide to Occupations in Science, Technology, Engineering, and Mathematics* (Progressive Careers). Indianapolis, IN: JIST Works, 2011.

Layne, Margaret. *Women in Engineering: Pioneers and Trailblazers.* Reston, VA: ASCE Press, 2009.

Layne, Margaret. *Women in Engineering: Professional Life.* Reston, VA: ASCE Press, 2009.

McCuen, Richard H., and Kristin L. Gilroy. *Ethics and Professionalism in Engineering.* Peterborough, ON, Canada: Broadview Press, 2010.

Millar, Dean C. *Ready for Takeoff! A Winning Process for Launching Your Engineering Career.* Upper Saddle River, NJ: Pearson Prentice Hall, 2011.

Parkinson, Claire L., Pamela S. Millar, and Michelle Thaller. *Women of Goddard: Careers in Science, Technology,*

Engineering & Mathematics. Greenbelt, MD: NASA Goddard Space Flight Center, 2011.

Peterson's Graduate Programs in Engineering & Applied Sciences 2014. Albany, NY: Peterson's Publishing, 2014.

Ritter, Arthur B., Vikki Hazelwood, Antonio Valdevit, and Alfred Ascione. *Biomedical Engineering Principles.* Boca Raton, FL: CRC Press, 2011.

Rosser, Sue Vilhauer. *Breaking into the Lab: Engineering Progress for Women in Science.* New York, NY: New York University Press, 2012.

Shatkin, Laurence. *Quick STEM Careers Guide: Four Steps to a Great Job in Science, Technology, Engineering, or Math* (Quick Job Series). Indianapolis, IN: JIST Works, 2011.

Wiles, Kelly. *Engineering, Mechanics, and Architecture.* New York, NY: Ferguson Publishing, 2010.

BIBLIOGRAPHY

A. James Clark School of Engineering, University of Maryland. "Undergraduate Program—Department of Civil & Environmental Engineering." 2013. Retrieved June 7, 2013 (http://www.civil.umd.edu/undergrad).

Associated Press. "Wearable Robots Getting Lighter, More Portable." INQUIRER.net, May 9, 2013. Retrieved June 30, 2013 (http://technology.inquirer.net/25233/wearable-robots-getting-lighter-more-portable).

Biello, David. "Plastic from Plants: Is It an Environmental Boon or Bane?" *Scientific American*, October 26, 2010. Retrieved August 5, 2013 (http://www.scientificamerican.com/article.cfm?id=is-plastic-from-plants-good-for-the-environment-or-bad).

Boscia, Ted. "Program Teaches Girls Engineering via Apparel Design." *Cornell Chronicle*, August 6, 2013. Retrieved August 7, 2013 (http://www.news.cornell.edu/stories/2013/08/program-teaches-girls-engineering-apparel-design).

Butterman, Eric. "Road Warrior Engineers." ASME.org, July 2013. Retrieved August 7, 2013 (https://www.asme.org).

Carnegie Mellon University. "Overview: Biomedical Engineering Major." June 9, 2011. Retrieved June 30, 2013 (http://www.bme.cmu.edu/ugprog/index.html).

Cornell University. "Curriculum and Courses—School of Chemical and Biomolecular Engineering." 2013. Retrieved June 7, 2013 (http://www.cheme.cornell.edu/cbe/academics/graduate/curriculum.cfm).

Discover Engineering in Greater Philadelphia. "Industrial Engineering." Retrieved June 30, 2013 (http://discoverengphila.org/disciplines/industrial).

Discover Engineering in Greater Philadelphia. "Material Science Engineering." Retrieved June 30, 2013 (http://discoverengphila.org/disciplines/materials).

Discover Engineering in Greater Philadelphia. "Mechanical Engineering." Retrieved June 30, 2013 (http://discoverengphila.org/disciplines/mechanical).

Engineers Without Borders. "Our History—Engineers Without Borders." 2013. Retrieved June 7, 2013 (http://www.ewb-usa.org/our-story/our-history).

Franklin Institute. "Cascading Influences: Long-Term Impacts of Informal STEM Experiences for Girls." March 2013. Retrieved August 11, 2013 (http://www.fi.edu/girls).

Girl Scouts of the USA. "Generation STEM: What Girls Say About Science, Technology, Engineering, and Math." 2012. Retrieved June 29, 2013 (http://www.girlscouts.org/research/publications/stem/generation_stem_what_girls_say.asp).

Haghi, A. K. *Recent Progress in Chemistry and Chemical Engineering Research.* New York, NY: Nova Science Publishers, 2010.

HuffingtonPost.com. "Ask a Physicist: 5 Tips for Women in Science." June 19, 2013. Retrieved June 29, 2013 (http://www.huffingtonpost.com/2013/06/19/the-traits-women-need-to-succeed-in-science_n_3416716.html?utm_hp_ref=girls-in-stem).

Hvistendahl, Mara. "China's Three Gorges Dam: An Environmental Catastrophe?" *Scientific American*, March 25, 2008. Retrieved May 6, 2013 (http://www.scientificamerican.com/article.cfm?id=chinas-three-gorges-dam-disaster).

Institution of Civil Engineers. "What Do Civil Engineers Do?" Retrieved June 20, 2013 (http://www.ice.org.uk/What-is-civil-engineering/What-do-civil-engineers-do).

Intel. "Intel Education—Intel Science Talent Search." 2013. Retrieved June 29, 2013 (http://www.intel.com/content/www/us/en/education/competitions/science-talent-search.html).

NASA. "Behind the Scenes: Engineering." July 1, 2009. Retrieved June 29, 2013. (http://spaceflight.nasa.gov/shuttle/support/engineering).

NASA. "NASA Engineering Network LLIS." 2013. Retrieved June 30, 2013 (http://llis.nasa.gov/llis/search/home.jsp).

National Engineers Week Foundation. "Types of Engineering." 2008. Retrieved October 28, 2013 (http://www.eweek.org/AboutEngineering/TypesEngineering.aspx).

Nei, Guo. "Three Gorges Dam Takes the First Strain." *China Daily*, June 6, 2006. Retrieved May 6, 2013 (http://www.chinadaily.com.cn/china/2006-06/06/content_609283.htm).

Nielsen, Stuart S. Interview with the author. July 24, 2013.

Parker Hannifin Corporation. "Indego Exoskeleton: The Future of Human Motion and Control."

2013. Retrieved June 10, 2013 (http://www.indego.com).

Saltzman, W. Mark. *Biomedical Engineering: Bridging Medicine and Technology*. New York, NY: Cambridge University Press, 2009.

ScienceGrrl. "News." 2013. Retrieved June 29, 2013 (http://sciencegrrl.co.uk/news).

Stanford University. "Undergraduate Students—Electrical Engineering." Retrieved June 7, 2013 (http://ee.stanford.edu/current-students/undergraduate-students).

Suh, Sang C., Varadraj P. Gurupur, and Murat Tanik. *Biomedical Engineering: Health Care Systems, Technology and Techniques*. New York, NY: Springer, 2011.

U.S. Bureau of Labor Statistics. "Electrical Engineers: Occupational Employment and Wages, May 2012." March 29, 2013. Retrieved June 20, 2013 (http://www.bls.gov/oes/current/oes172071.htm).

White House. "Women in STEM." Retrieved June 29, 2013 (http://www.whitehouse.gov/administration/eop/ostp/women).

INDEX

A

About the Author

Published author Gina Hagler writes about science and technology on her blog, *Synthesis*. Her books for Springer Verlag are about engineering-related topics. She has taught and led training workshops in the STEM fields and has developed curriculum for a variety of STEM courses. She is a member of the National Association of Science Writers (NASW) and the American Society of Journalists and Authors (ASJA).

Photo Credits

Cover, p. 1 Matt Cardy/Getty Images; pp. 4–5 Liu Jin/AFP/ Getty Images; pp. 10, 12, 16–17, 21, 28, 36–37, 38–39, 46–47, 60, 62, 64–65, 80, 82–83, 88–89, 92, 102, 108 © AP Images; pp. 22–23 Hyoung Chang/The Denver Post/Getty Images; pp. 26–27 Boris Horvat/AFP/Getty Images; pp. 34–35 Chicago Tribune/McClatchy-Tribune/Getty Images; pp. 40–41 Boston Globe/Getty Images; pp. 48–49, 52–53, 76–77 The Washington Post/Getty Images; p. 57 DTE Energy/AP Images; p. 66 Joe Raedle/ Getty Images; p. 71 Ron Felt/Georgia Tech/AP Images; pp. 78–79 RJ Sangosti/The Denver Post/Getty Images; p. 84 Helen H. Richardson/The Denver Post/Getty Images; p. 93 Danny Moloshok/Reuters/Landov; p. 96 Wavebreak Media/Thinkstock; pp. 100–101 Imaginechina/AP Images; pp. 104–105 Joe Amon/ The Denver Post/Getty Images; p. 106 South Dakota State University/AP Images. Cover and interior design: elements © iStockphoto.com/kemie, iStock/Thinkstock, © iStockphoto .com/julioechandia, © iStockphoto.com/alwyncooper.

Designer: Brian Garvey; Editor: Andrea Sclarow Paskoff; Photo Researcher: Amy Feinberg